The Lee-on-the-Solent Railway

Peter A. Harding

A general view of the platform at Lee-on-the-Solent Station, with former LB&SCR "Terrier" A1X
No.B661 and a single 'gate' carriage on February 14th 1928.   H.C.Casserley

Published by

Peter A. Harding
"Mossgiel", Bagshot Road, Knaphill,
Woking, Surrey GU21 2SG.
ISBN 978 0 9552403 7 9
© Peter A. Harding 2012.
Printed by Binfield Print & Design Ltd.,
Binfield Road, Byfleet Village, Surrey KT14 7PN.

Contents

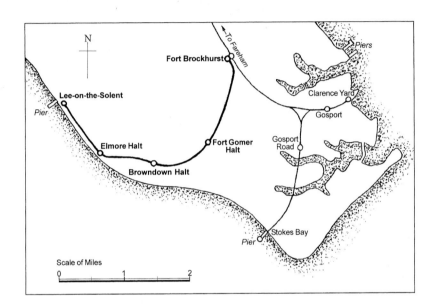

LSWR 0-6-0ST No.392 at Lee-on-the-Solent Station. This locomotive was built by Manning Wardle and was formally called "Lady Portsmouth" but, after a visit to Nine Elms in 1885 for a new boiler the name was left off and not replaced.

Lens of Sutton

Introduction

The Lee-on-the-Solent Railway was an important part of the development of Lee-on-the-Solent as a seaside resort in the latter part of the 19th century. The development began in the 1880's when Charles Newton-Robinson saw the potential of the area and persuaded his father Sir John Charles Robinson to provide the funds for purchasing the land and setting up the Lee-on-the-Solent Estates Company.

Over the next ten years the town was established, beginning with the building of the Marine Parade and then the pier. Following on from the pier, the next part of the development was to form the Lee-on-the-Solent Railway to connect with the national railway network at Fort Brockhurst on the main line between Fareham and Gosport. This was achieved on Saturday May 12th 1894 when the line opened to the public and on Thursday May 31st 1894 when Countess Clanwilliam (daughter of Sir Arthur Kennedy and wife of Richard Meade, 4th Earl of Clanwilliam, the Naval Commander-in-Chief of Portsmouth) carried out the formal opening of the new railway.

Unfortunately, during the early part of the 20th century the railway was not really turning out to be a great success and was losing money. Although the London & South Western Railway had worked the line since 1909, they never actually owned it. After the 1923 grouping, both the London & South Western Railway and the Lee-on-the-Solent Railway were absorbed into the newly formed Southern Railway who later decided to close the line to passengers on January 1st 1931 and then to goods on September 30th 1935, although the last goods train ran on October 2nd 1935.

Former LB&SCR D1 class 0-4-2T No.B239 and LSWR 'gate' set No.374 with an open wagon and box van wait at the platform at Lee-on-the-Solent on December 31st 1930, the last day of public service although, D1 class 0-4-2T No.B626 worked the final run. *Portsmouth Evening News*

3

History of the Line

Situated on the coast of the Solent and forming part of the borough of Gosport, Lee-on-the-Solent is today a small pleasant seaside resort which has an interesting past of great hopes for a bright future which never really materialised.

The very existence of Lee-on-the-Solent owes much to Mr.Charles Newton-Robinson who while on a yachting cruise on the Solent during the 1880's saw that the very position of what was then practically an uninhabited area with just a few isolated cottages and farm buildings, had the potential of developing into a seaside resort to rival somewhere like Bournemouth or Southsea. He passed on his idea to his father, Sir John Charles Robinson who was a wealthy artist and art connoisseur who soon agreed with his son and was able to finance the Lee-on-the-Solent Estates Company to develop the new resort. Until then this area had been at various times known as Ly, Le Breton and Lee Brittain.

Charles Newton-Robinson (the name Newton coming from his mothers maiden name) was the eldest son of Sir John Charles Robinson, and although a barrister by profession was a man of many talents who apart from his love of yachting, shared his fathers interest for collecting art and was also a poet and writer who later was a member of the British fencing team and won a silver medal at the 1906 Olympic Games in Athens.

As mentioned, Sir John Charles Robinson, CB, FSA was a wealthy gentleman artist who did not depend on the sale of his work to provide an income. Originally a painter of landscapes and flowers and trained in Paris, he later became more well known as an organiser, teacher, critic and collector of art. For 17 years he was Superintendent of the Art Collections at the Victoria and Albert Museum from when it was originally founded as the South Kensington Museum in 1852. He later reached the prestigious position of Surveyor of Queen Victoria's pictures, a post he held for nearly 20 years until the death of the Queen in 1901. For many years he lived in Harley Street in London before later moving to Newton Manor at Swanage in Dorset.

Building operations for the Lee-on-the-Solent Estates Company which Sir John Charles Robinson financed to develop the area soon commenced and quickly converted what was basically a barren waste where over the years some digging of gravel had taken place into a charming little residential resort, where it was said that those who wish to spend their holidays "far from the madding crowd" can do so. The Marine Parade which runs parallel with the sea for over a mile and separated from the sea by a 150 ft wide grass strip was one of the first features to be built while foundations for new neatly laid out housing developments and roads quickly followed.

Sir John Charles Robinson
(1824-1913)

As an up and coming seaside resort, it was soon decided that what was required to rival places like Bournemouth and Southsea was a pier which always seemed to delight the Victorians and of which could provide a possible steamer link with the Isle of Wight, Portsmouth, Southsea and Southampton plus and perhaps even more importantly, a railway to connect with the nearby national railway network.

Powers for a 750 ft iron pier were obtained in 1885 to the design of Messrs. Galbraith and Church to replace a small wooden jetty which stood on the shore in the same position. Sir John Charles Robinson personally financed the £8,500 cost of erecting the pier and in July of that year, his wife Lady Robinson unveiled the foundation stone. The contractor appointed to carry out the construction was Mr.F.Bevis of St.Thomas's Street, Portsmouth who started the work in 1886 and by the autumn of 1887 the work was completed apart from the entrance building which was erected by Mr.Wareham of Titchfield for a cost of £334. The pier was approached from Marine Drive and later came to house a small pavilion known as the Golden Hall and a bandstand. In autumn 1887, Sir John Charles Robinson formed the Lee-on-the-Solent Pier Company with a capital of £12,500 in £5 shares to fund it. Unfortunately the share capital was slow to be taken up and the pier remained the virtual personal property of Sir John Charles Robinson. The pier was actually opened on April 3rd 1888 and having previously unveiled the foundation stone, Lady Robinson was now able to perform the opening ceremony.

The Lee-on-the-Solent Pier.   Authors Collection

The next major project was to connect with the nearby national railway network by the formation of the Lee-on-the-Solent Railway Company. The original promoters first looked at a line to run direct from Fareham to Lee-on-the-Solent through Titchfield and Crofton (which was later engulfed by Stubbington) and even put in a provisional application for powers on November 15th 1888 to build it, but, later settled for a light basic railway from a bay platform at Fort Brockhurst on the Fareham to Gosport main line (which had opened on February 7th 1842) with possible stopping places in between at Pound Lane, Privett, Browndown and Elmore. Mr.R.H.Tigg was engaged by the Company to carry out a survey for the building of the line.

Mr.Tigg carried out the survey and estimated the costs for construction of the 3 miles 8 chains line would be £18,684 with £1,868 8s for contingencies. Although sufficient land was to be obtained for later doubling the line if required, the original idea was to get things moving by laying a line of flat bottom steel rails of 60lb secured by dog spikes on cross sleepers. It was also proposed to work the line with American type tramcar carriages with low steps at each end which meant that low platforms at the in between stopping places would be all that was required with standard platforms at Lee-on-the-Solent and Fort Brockhurst only.

5

With some idea of how much the construction was going to cost, the next step was to obtain powers to actually build the line. As the undertaking was to be a light basic railway, it unfortunately pre-dated the Light Railway Act of 1896, so an application was made to the Board of Trade on June 14th 1889 under the little used Railway Construction Facilities Act of 1864. Nearly a year later, the *Portsmouth Evening News* of June 6th 1890 briefly announced the following short statement:

LEE-ON-THE-SOLENT
The Lee-on-the-Solent Railway Bill has passed unopposed through Parliament.

Although the line was sanctioned as the Lee-on-the-Solent (Light) Railway, under the Railway Construction Facilities Act of 1864, the Board of Trade insisted on full railway requirements of crossing gates, fencing etc which added to the cost although, as the line was to be run as a 'one engine in steam' line, no signals were required. The Hundred of Manhood & Selsey Tramway in Sussex was also sanctioned by this same Act.

The *London Gazette* of July 11th 1890 saw the publication of the certificate which was dated July 5th 1890 incorporating the company with a capital of £30,000 in £10 shares. The first board of directors were the original promoters Charles Edward Morgan, Charles Langley Whetham, James Edward Hunter, William Stephens Cross and Harry Emans Pollard. The Company Secretary was Mr.G.A.Petter.

Messrs. David Laing & Son of London were appointed contractors for the construction and equipping the line for £24,375 in November 1890 while Mr.F.Gillham was appointed engineer.

The ceremony of turning the first sod took place on Wednesday October 22nd 1890 at the site of the terminus of the new railway at Lee-on-the-Solent which was situated near the pier. The ceremony was performed by Harry Emans Pollard who by now was the Chairman of the Board. At the invitation of Sir John Charles Robinson, all those present were entertained at a champagne luncheon in the Assembly Rooms at the Victoria Hotel, at which Charles Newton-Robinson presided.

It appears that nothing much had been done by April 1891 and at this time Mr.Gillham informed the Board that he would be working abroad for a while and then on November 17th 1891 he wrote to the Board and told them that he was in fact resigning. This naturally didn't go down too well with the Board who wanted things to move as quickly as possible.

With very little happening and the Railway Company getting very restless, Charles Newton-Robinson informed the Board in November 1892 that his father Sir John Charles Robinson had offered to come to the rescue once again by obtaining the remaining unsold shares of the capital of the Company. This enabled a new contractor to be employed and in early 1893 Messrs. Pauling & Elliott of Westminster were approached and agreed to take over the construction of the line while in February 1893, Mr.P.W.Meik was appointed as consulting engineer. Patrick Meik was from a family of engineers which included his father Thomas and his brother Charles. He was very experienced and had been involved as resident engineer on such contracts as the construction of the foundations and piers for the Forth Rail Bridge.

For the construction of the line, Messrs. Pauling & Elliott brought with them two standard gauge locos, a Manning Wardle 0-4-0 saddle tank No.334 called "Stanley" and a Manning Wardle 0-4-0 saddle tank No.156 (sometimes described as a 0-6-0) which at one time carried the name "Sylph" when it was previously owned by Logan Hemingway.

It seems that the work was well on its way by the spring of 1893 at which time Mr.James Willing, jun was now Chairman of the Company and about a 100 men had been employed on the job from the first week in March although the marshy soil near the small River Alver (which the line crossed over between Privett and Browndown), did slow things down for a while.

6

As the Railway Company wanted their line to be opened as soon as possible they requested that the Board of Trade inspect the work done. The inspection was carried out by Major Yorke for the Board of Trade on July 15th 1893. Unfortunately, Major Yorke reported that the line failed his inspection on thirteen points, the main things seemed to be that gauge ties were required on any curves of less than 15ch radius. He also mentioned that the line appeared to be partly built outside the limits of deviation set and added that the gradients were steeper than those originally proposed.

This news no doubt annoyed the Railway Company and with the knowledge that they had already obtained two tramway style bogie carriages with longitudinal seats and end platforms which were built by Brown Marshalls of Birmingham, the engineer Mr.P.W.Meik suggested to the Board of Trade that the line could be opened in its present state as a tramroad, unfortunately, this proposal quickly received a sharp refusal.

During the early part of 1894 many of the requested changes had been completed which now included standard height platforms at all the stopping places as well as providing a porter. On March 28th 1894 the Railway Company wrote to the Board of Trade informing them that the line would be ready for another inspection the following month. A further letter was sent on April 7th stating that they wished to open the line on April 28th 1894, and that the two American or tramcar-type carriages have now been fitted with continuous footboards at the same height as ordinary carriages.

Despite the request for an April 28 1894 opening, the re-inspection was not carried out until May 7th 1894 by Major Yorke who mentioned in his report that there are now small corrugated iron gatekeeper's cabins at each level crossing, each with a clock, stove, seat and table. He also said that there is no longer the intention to use Pound Lane or Elmore as stopping places and added that the following needed to be carried out:-

1. Buffers at Brockhurst on the siding between the LSWR and the Lee-on-the-Solent Railway Company.
2. Platform ramps are too steep.
3. Fencing needed at the rear of Privett and Browndown stations.
4. A 10 mph maximum speed as agreed by the Company.

A provisional sanction was given for the opening with a further re-inspection at a later date to make sure that the changes had been completed.

This news no doubt pleased the Board who had taken steps to make sure that the railway opened smoothly by employing the experienced Mr.E.B.Ivatts as railway manager .

After the provisional sanction to open the line had been given by Major Yorke, the following article appeared in the Wednesday May 9th 1894 edition of the *Portsmouth Evening News*:-

THE NEW LEE-ON-THE-SOLENT RAILWAY
We are officially informed that the Lee-on-the-Solent Railway was inspected on Monday by the Board of Trade Inspector, Major Yorke, and has been passed for opening. It is expected to be opened for passenger traffic for Whitsuntide, of which due notification will be given. Six trains will start from Fort Brockhurst Station to Lee-on-the-Solent, and six from Lee to Fort Brockhurst during the day, between the hours of 8.30 a.m. and 8.30 p.m. There will also be through day return tickets issued by the Floating Bridge Company at Portsmouth to convey passengers across the ferry, thence by tram to Station Road, Brockhurst, and forward by train from Fort Brockhurst Station to Lee, the same facility being afforded for the Lee people to journey to Portsmouth and back. Passengers can join or leave the trains at Privett or Browndown, as the trains will be stopped at these places by signal or on notice being given to the guard. On Sundays there will be five trains running between Fort Brockhurst and Lee-on-the-Solent, commencing at 1.50 p.m. from Fort Brockhurst, and the last leaving Lee at 8.00 p.m.

☙ RAILWAY COMMUNICATION ❧

WITH

LEE-ON-THE-SOLENT.

....

By reference to the Map of the District it will be seen that there are at present no less than Four Railway Stations within easy reach of LEE-ON-THE-SOLENT by Road, namely—

Stokes Bay (3 miles), Fareham (4½ miles), Brockhurst (2½ miles), and Gosport Road.

Fast Trains run to Fareham Station from Waterloo in two hours and twenty minutes.

Communication is kept up twice daily (except Sundays) throughout the year with Fareham Station by Omnibus.

The Fareham and Netley Railway, constructed by the L. & S.W. Railway Company, has brought Lee-on-the-Solent into direct communication with Southampton, *via* Fareham.

But the existing Railway facilities will be greatly improved by the making of the New

Lee-on-the-Solent Railway

From BROCKHURST STATION of the L. & S.W. Railway Co. to LEE-ON-THE-SOLENT, where there is a Terminal Station close to the Pier

Brockhurst is connected with Gosport by an existing Tramway.

Publicity material for the forthcoming new railway to Lee-on-the-Solent.

Although the formal opening of the line did not take place until Thursday May 31st 1894, the line did in fact open for passengers on Saturday May 12th 1894 just in time for Whit Monday. The train for the first few weeks was made up of the two tramway style bogie carriages which the Company owned and were built by Brown Marshalls of Birmingham, and a Manning Wardle 0-6-0ST locomotive called "Jumbo" which was "on loan" from the London & South Western Railway (LSWR). The *Hampshire Telegraph and Sussex Chronicle* reported the opening in their Saturday May 19th 1894 edition:-

LEE-ON-THE-SOLENT AND ITS NEW RAILWAY

Lee-on-the-Solent is a proud, little watering place today. It has a railway line of its own connecting it with that outer world to which it must look for development. Opened on Saturday, the new line, which runs its level length of three miles from Lee to Fort Brockhurst, is now in good working trim. It had a foretaste of the busy season to come on Whit Monday, when over a thousand excursionists availed themselves of the opportunity it afforded to visit the pretty resort which so pleasantly combines rural with seaside beauties, and many more had to be left behind because the cars were "full up". We say cars advisedly, for the vehicles that run behind the shunting engine which draws the train are more like tramcars in appearance than like the carriages one is accustomed to see on the larger railways. They are built on the American plan, with long seats running parallel with the lines of rail and with a platform at each end, on which the passenger may stand and inhale the fresh air as he views the surrounding scenery. There are two halting places along the line. One is at Privett, and the other - most convenient for marksmen - at Browndown. But the train only stops at these platforms when there are passengers to take up or set down. On week days the train runs half-a-dozen journeys each way over the single line of rails, and on Sundays five journeys are performed each way. This is as much as the traffic demands at present, but if occasion requires there is no reason why "Jumbo" as the line engine is named, should not be called upon to work a little oftener. One day we may see an "Alice" to bear him company on a double line. There is no undue haste on "Jumbo's" part for the Board of Trade regulations do not allow of a greater speed than ten miles an hour, and the passenger who traverse the route for pleasure has a good opportunity of seeing about him on the twenty minutes' journey.

It is neither a difficult nor costly business to get to Lee now. The beneficent penny-a-mile system obtains for third-class passengers between Lee and Fort Brockhurst, while the luxury of second-class may be had for sixpence, and that of first class for ninepence. Thanks largely to the friendly personal relations which exist between Mr.E.B.Ivatts, the manager of the new Railway Company, and Mr.Scotter, the general manager of the South-Western Company, through bookings to Lee have been arranged from London and the principal stations on the South-Western line.

The report also mentions that Portsmouth people could get to Lee with the minimum of outlay. For tenpence a third-class day return ticket from Portsmouth covers the Floating Bridge (a steam-powered floating bridge, guided by chains) to Gosport and then the tramway from High Street, Gosport to Fort Brockhurst, and then the train to Lee and back by the same route. The report also pointed out that the following week a steam launch service would commence running between Southsea Clarence Esplanade pier to Lee-on-the-Solent pier, so that day trippers may, if they choose, go by water and return by rail or vice versa. There was also a possibility that a direct tram line from Gosport could be built to Privett which would make the journey between Gosport and Lee just twenty minutes.

The report continues as follows:

As Lee-on-the-Solent gets better known its residential and holiday advantages cannot well fail to become generally appreciated. To make it better known is the chief business of the railway management, which is in the hands of an experienced pilot in Mr. Ivatts. He has been engaged in railway work in India, in Ireland, and at home, and not alone for that reason may he be described as a man of parts. What responsible railway official has not heard of Ivatt's "Carriers Law" and "Railway Management"? The former work - a bulky volume comprising digests of law cases dating from the time of the Stuarts - and has to be regarded as a railway text-book, and has afforded the basis of more than one decision given by the Recorder of Dublin in matters of railway law. The other is of equal value to responsible railway officials. Mr. Ivatts is only a bird of passage at Lee, and will probably take his flight when he has accomplished his mission of setting the new line on its legs - or should one say on its rails? Well, the railway will bring the people to Lee, and when they get there they will have a pleasant time. The residents - not very numerous at present, but select - slightly invert the Christian maxim by being of the world, but not in it. About them they find such surroundings of modern civilisation as a pier, an hotel, with a lawn-tennis ground and a commodious assembly-room attached, and a bathing machine; and withal they are out of the busy world, and with the sea on one side and the rural beauties of nature on the other, dwell in a lotus land of calm delight. Daisies and buttercups are strewn around, the lark sings merrily high in the air, and the sweet rich notes of the cuckoo and the nightingale are not wanting to complete the attraction.

The report concluded as follows:

But time flies, and the train is going. "All aboard" : and off she glides, amid friendly farewells, past the busily working windmill that draws from a well within a few yards of the shore the supplies of fresh water that are necessary for the engine; on to Browndown, where the tented field presents to the eye a microcosm of that "armed camp of Europe" about which after dinner orators are so fond of talking when they respond for "The Army". A youth stands on the Browndown platform, calmly holding a red flag, at sight of which the train comes to a

9

halt, and allows a red-coated marksman, who has been class-firing at the butts to step on. Then off again, until Privett is reached, where another red flag is waved, and another stop made to take up a lady. A few more leisurely puffs, and we are at Fort Brockhurst Station, close to the tram which is to carry us away from the pleasant association of Lee-on-the-Solent and its railway line into the busy world of Gosport.

As previously mentioned, the formal opening of the line was not until Thursday May 31st 1894 and once again "Jumbo" the Manning Wardle 0-6-0ST pulled the two tramway style bogie carriages. This very eventful day was covered by the *Portsmouth Evening News* in their Friday June 1st 1894 edition:-

LEE-ON-THE-SOLENT
FORMAL OPENING OF THE RAILWAY

Though trains have been running for a fortnight on the new railway from Brockhurst to Lee-on-the-Solent, the official opening of the line did not take place till Thursday, when it was attended with considerable *éclat*. A special train from Waterloo brought most of the guests to Brockhurst, whence they conveyed over the new line to Lee. Others proceeded from Southsea by steam launch. The party were received at the station by Mr.C.Newton-Robinson, and Mr.Ivatts, the manager, the band of the South Wales Borderers being also in attendance. The station, as indeed, the whole place, was gaily decorated with flags, which also fluttered from the train. Shortly after the arrival the assembly was joined by the Countess of Clanwilliam, with the Ladies Meade and Flag-Lieutenant Munday, Sir John Charles Robinson and Lady Robinson (on whose estate the new watering place is built), Sir Frederick FitzWygram and the Mayor and Mayoress of Portsmouth (Alderman and Mrs.A.L.Emanuel). The Countess of Clanwilliam was presented with a handsome shower bouquet of orchids and roses by Master Till, and Lady Robinson was handed another by Master Hannen. The principal guests next took their places on a small platform, and the Revs. Pitt (Vicar of Crofton) and Prideaux-Brune (Rector of Rowner) performed a short service, with the help of a choir.

The special party of guests who assembled at Lee-on-the-Solent Station to celebrate the formal opening of the railway on Thursday May 31st 1894.   Author's Collection

Sir F. FitzWygram then thanked Lady Clanwilliam for her presence there. He said that the South of England had long been a resort for people who wanted to restore themselves to health, but most of the watering places on the south coast were old towns, and not so good as new ones. They had narrow streets, and the drainage was generally bad. But Lee-on-the-Solent was a new place. It had all sorts of attractions for visitors. He must admit that the line of railway was not pretty, but that was all the better when they got there and saw the splendid views. He thought there was a great future before Lee-on-the-Solent, because it started with power for development. He could confidently recommend it to everybody as a health resort. (Applause).

Mr. Ivatts then gave the Countess a key of the station, and she declared the line open.

The visitors presently wended their way to the Victoria Hotel, in the assembly room of which Mr.F.H.Hannen, the host, served a *recherche* luncheon. Besides the ladies and gentlemen already mentioned, the company included Admiral and Miss DeKantzow, Mr. and Mrs. James Willing, jun. (Chairman of Directors), Colonel C. Mumby (Chairman of the Gosport Local Board), Mr.James Lemon (ex-Mayor of Southampton), and various leading officials of the South Western Railway. - After lunch the toast list was commenced with the "Health of the Queen", proposed by Sir John Charles Robinson. Mr.W.S.J.Wilde next proposed the health and happiness of Sir John Charles Robinson and Lady Robinson, without whom, he said, the event for which they were gathered would never have come to pass. There was no question that Lee-on-the-Solent was a very healthful, airy, place. The railway appeared to be very well laid, and everything ran very smoothly.

Sir John Charles Robinson thanked them for the honour. He remarked that it was difficult for him to realise the full import of the matter which had brought them together. When he remembered that ten years ago the place was nothing but a lone, out-lying farm by the sea-side, tenauted only by sheep, cows, pigs, and a few rustics devoted in bringing up the animals, he could scarcely realise that it had become a town which was the first sight on which the eyes of the Queen rested in her island home. His two sons had taken the chief part in the undertaking, and to them was undoubtedly due most of the success. It had been a very arduous undertaking, endless difficulties had had to be grappled with and overcome - so great, indeed, that he had been more than once tempted to ask himself whether it was not a crime to build a new railway in England. However, as they saw, they had managed to pull through at last.

Manning Wardle 0-6-0ST "Jumbo" with the two tramway style carriages at the bay platform at Fort Brockhurst Station on Thursday May 31st 1894, the formal opening day of the new line. John Alsop Collection

Mr. Charles Newton-Robinson gave "The Visitors" coupling with the toast the name of the Mayor of Portsmouth. - Alderman Emanuel, in responding, alluded with regret to the approaching departure of the Earl and Countess of Clanwilliam. As chief Magistrate of the Borough of Portsmouth, he said that the Countess was beloved in the town and would ever be remembered. They in Portsmouth wished Lee every success. He must take exception to the remarks of Sir F. FitzWygram as to bad drains. In Southsea they had nothing to complain of in that respect.

Mr.Louis Till proposed "The Lee-on-the-Solent Railway", and said the Board of Directors was sparing no trouble or expense to make the line a success, and the manager was doing his utmost to make it an attraction. - Mr.James Willing, Jun., cordially thanked the company for the compliment.

LEE-ON-THE-SOLENT RAILWAY

Through booking from Waterloo and other L. & S.W.R. Stations to Lee-on-the-Solent by the

❋ NEW RAILWAY ❋

Which was opened for traffic on Saturday, 12th May, 1894. It commences at Brockhurst Station, L. & S.W. Railway Co., and ends at a terminal station at Lee-on-the-Solent, close to the Pier, and almost on the Beach.

TIME TABLE.

Trains from Fort Brockhurst (L. & S.W.) to Lee-on-the-Solent.

		a.m.	a.m.	a.m.	a.m.	p.m.	p.m.
London (Waterloo)	dep.	5 50	6 9	9 15	11 15	2 25	4 55
Basingstoke	,,	7 8	...	10 33	12 35	3 33	6 8
Winchester	,,	7 35	8 25	10 59	1 8	4 3	6 37
Southampton	,,	7 20	8 25	10 50	1 5	3 50	6 30
Eastleigh	,,	7 52	9 5	11 25	1 40	4 18	6 55
Fareham	arr.	8 13	9 27	11 46	2 2	4 35	7 21
Fareham	dep.	8 16	9 53	11 47	2 10	4 37	7 25
Fort Brockhurst Junction	arr.	8 24	10 1	11 55	2 18	4 44	7 33
Ryde	dep.	...	9 0	...	1 55	4 0	6 15
Stokes Bay	,,	...	9 30	...	2 30	4 28	6 40
Gosport Road (Alverstoke)	,,	...	9 34	...	2 34	4 32	6 44
		a.m.					
Gosport	,,	8 12	...	...	...	...	6 53
Fort Brockhurst Junction	arr.	8 16	9 39	...	2 38	4 36	6 57
		a.m.	a.m.	p.m.	p.m.	p.m.	p.m.
Fort Brockhurst Junct.	dep.	8 30	10 15	12 0	2 50	4 50	7 45
Privett	,,	...	...	to	stop	by	signal
Browndown	,,	...	...		ditto		
Lee-on-the-Solent	,,	8 50	10 35	12 20	3 10	5 10	8 5

Trains from Lee-on-the-Solent to Fort Brockhurst (L. & S.W.)

		a.m.	a.m.	p.m.	p.m.	p.m.	p.m.
Lee-on-the-Solent	dep.	9 10	11 30	1 50	4 8	6 30	8 20
Browndown	,,	...	to	stop	by	signal	...
Privett	,,	...	...	ditto	...	...	...
Fort Brockhurst Junct.	arr.	9 30	11 50	2 10	4 28	6 50	8 40
Fort Brockhurst Junction	dep.	9 39	...	2 38	4 36	6 57	9 14
Fareham	arr.	9 47	...	2 46	4 43	7 6	9 21
Fareham	dep.	9 57	...	2 50	4 48	7 12	9 26
Eastleigh	,,	10 28	...	3 31	5 30	7 42	10 5
Winchester	,,	10 43	...	3 46	5 45	7 57	10 20
Southampton	,,	10 43	...	3 42	5 49	8 1	10 7
Basingstoke	,,	11 13	...	4 21	6 23	8 37	...
London (Waterloo)	,,	12 18	...	5 42	7 31	9 50	...
		a.m.	a.m.	p.m.	p.m.	p.m.	
Fort Brockhurst Junction	dep.	10	1 55	2 18	4 41	7 33	8 45
Gosport	arr.	10 5	11 59	...	...	7 37	8 49
Gosport Road (Alverstoke)	,,	10 29	...	2 23	4 47	...	...
Stokes Bay	,,	10 33	...	2 27	4 50	...	...
Ryde	,,	11 0	...	2 55	5 15	...	...

SUNDAY TRAINS.

		a.m.				
London (Waterloo)	dep.	10 15	...	...	...	...
Basingstoke	,,	12 5	...	...	...	...
Winchester	,,	12 40	...	...	...	...
Southampton	,,	12 40	...	...	...	...
Eastleigh	,,	1 3	...	...	...	...
Fareham	arr.	1 29	...	...		
					p.m.	
Fareham	dep.	1 32	...	...	6 0	
Fort Brockhurst Junction	arr.	1 42	...	...	6 10	
Ryde		...	...	...		
Stokes Bay		...	...	...		
Gosport Road (Alverstoke)						
		p.m.				
Gosport	dep.	1 10	...	5 25	7 15	
Fort Brockhurst Junction	arr.	1 15	...	5 30	7 20	
		p.m.	p.m.	p.m.	p.m.	p.m.
Fort Brockhurst Junct.	dep.	1 50	3 0	4	5 35	7 25
Privett	,,	...	to	stop	by	signal
Browndown	,,			ditto		
Lee-on-the-Solent	arr.	2 10	3 20	4 20	5 50	7 40

SUNDAY TRAINS.

		p.m.	p.m.	p.m.	p.m.	p.m.
Lee-on-the-Solent	dep.	2 30	3 30	5 0	6 55	8 0
Browndown	,,	...	to	stop	by	signal
Privett	,,	...	...	ditto	...	...
Fort Brockhurst Junct.	arr.	2 50	3 50	5 20	7 10	8 20
Fort Brockhurst Junction	dep.	...	...	5 30	7 20	...
Fareham	arr.	...	...	5 39	7 29	...
Fareham	dep.	...	...	5 45	7 36	...
Eastleigh	,,	...	...	6 22	8 5	...
Winchester	,,	...	...	6 39	8 20	...
Southampton	,,	...	...	6 32	8 27	...
Basingstoke	,,	...	...	7 18	8 50	...
London (Waterloo)	,,	...	...	8 51	10 1	...
		p.m.				p.m.
Fort Gosport Junction	dep.	6 10	...			8 48
Gosport	arr.	6 15	...			8 53
Gosport Road (Alverstoke)	,,					
Stokes Bay	,,					
Ryde	,,					

N.B.—The times of arrival and departure of L. & S.W. Trains at Fort Brockhurst and other stations are given here, but the Lee-on-the-Solent Co. do not hold themselves responsible for same

Colonel C. Mumby proposed "Lee-on-the-Solent" which, he said, had been founded through the perseverance of Sir John Charles Robinson. He wished it every success. Everything which tended to the good of Lee re-acted favourably on Gosport, and he was sure there was a future before the place. - Mr.C.Newton-Robinson responded, and said the people of neighbouring towns had shown their practical belief in the place by purchasing land there. (Applause).

This concluded the speech-making. The party then broke up, and excursions were made to the beach, pier, & co. Shortly after five o'clock they embarked on the train for Brockhurst, and were soon in the special, for Waterloo and speeding away from the pleasant watering-place.

After the formal opening, the line soon settled down to an everyday existence and on November 5th 1894 a further re-inspection was carried out for the Board of Trade by the then recently promoted Lt.Col.Yorke. This re-inspection had been promised when the provisional opening was sanctioned on May 7th 1894 and on this occasion Lt.Col.Yorke noted that all the pending work had been carried out and he was now happy to fully sanction the line with a proviso that the Company keep a watchful eye on the banks of two of the bridges which the line crossed. As previously mentioned, during the lines construction, the marshy soil near the bridge over the small River Alver did slow things down for a while, although by abolishing the original larger bridge and diverting part of the river by making two courses with two similar bridges helped to ease this problem.

After the re-inspection it must be assumed that the speed limit was increased to 15 mph as during 1895 the Company requested that the limit be increased from 15 mph to 20 mph. This request was approved on the condition that gauge ties were fitted on some of the curves and that continuous brakes were added to the carriages.

Unfortunately, the Company were not making the amount of money in the first few years that the Board had hoped for, and sometimes barely covered the staff wages. With the financial situation causing some concern, there appears to have been some interest shown by the LSWR in February 1896 of a possible takeover but nothing happened and the Lee-on-the-Solent Company continued under its own management.

The finances had slightly improved by 1898 and there was even talk of the Company buying their own locomotive but, they later decided against this idea and would continue to hire from the LSWR.

An early view of the station at Lee-on-the-Solent taken from the pier showing just how close to the beach the station was.   Lens of Sutton

13

During the early days of the line, the regular locomotive hired to the Company from the LSWR was 2-4-0T No.21 "Scott" which was built by George England in 1861and is recorded as taking over from the Manning Wardle built 0-6-0ST "Jumbo" in May 1894. Later when the LSWR were using 2-4-0T "Scott" elsewhere, another Manning Wardle locomotive 0-6-0ST No.392 formally called "Lady Portsmouth" was used.

As expected, once the line was up and running, the line's manager Mr.E.B.Ivatts did take flight after his mission was accomplished and was replaced by another one of Sir John Charles Robinson sons Mr. Edmund A. Robinson who had been involved with the railway with his brother Charles Newton-Robinson from the start.

Over the following few years the line was once more running at a loss with goods traffic particularly poor. As they owed money to the LSWR it seems that they living in the hope that the LSWR would purchase the line and all their troubles would be over. In fact in 1903 it was agreed that the LSWR would advertise the line in their timetables and carriages but still no further talk of a takeover.

In June 1908 the LSWR said that the two locomotives which had been loaned to the Company were worn out and that they had no other locomotives which were suitable for this particular line. However, the LSWR were always willing to help and suggested that their H13 Steam Railcars could operate the line without to many difficulties but, before such a change happened, as from July 26th 1909 the LSWR made financial arrangements to in fact operate the line but were very careful not to actually buy it so the Lee-on-the-Solent Railway remained nominally independent.

Under the influence of the LSWR one of the first things that happened was in October 1909 when the platform at Privett was re-name Fort Gomer as it was felt that the name confused passengers with Privett Station on the LSWR's Meon Valley line between Alton and Eastleigh. Fort Gomer was the name of a nearby Victorian fort which with other forts in the district were built in the 1860's as a defence for Portsmouth and the surrounding area from any possible attack from France. They were commissioned and implemented by the then Prime Minister Lord Henry Palmerston and were known locally as Palmerston's Folly.

The arrival on the platform at Browndown of General Franklin to review an un-identified brigade c.1908.
John Alsop Collection

With the H13 Steam Railcars in use, the platforms at Fort Gomer and Browndown which had previously been described as stations or just sometimes platforms were from then on referred to as halts or sometimes 'Rail Motor Halts' and on April 11th 1910 a new halt was opened at Elmore which was between Browndown and Lee-on-the-Solent and had been mentioned as a possible stopping place when the line was first suggested.

The tramway from Gosport to Privett which was mentioned earlier in the *Hampshire Telegraph and Sussex Chronicle* of the Saturday May 19th 1894 after the original opening to passengers never materialised, and no doubt much to the relief of the Lee-on-the-Solent Railway Company nor did a further suggestion of a tramway from Gosport to Lee-on-the-Solent.

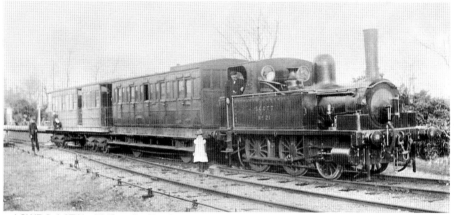

LSWR 2-4-0T No.21 "Scott" at Fort Brockhurst ready to leave for Lee-on-the-Solent on December 26th 1900.
Pamlin Prints

LSWR 0-6-0ST No.392 formally called "Lady Portsmouth" also at Fort Brockhurst at a simlar time.
Lens of Sutton

15

On April 10th 1913 saw the death of Sir John Charles Robinson at the age of 88 and then just eleven days later on April 21st 1913 sadly his eldest son Charles Newton-Robinson also passed away, aged 60. These two gentlemen were the main instigators for not only the Lee-on-the-Solent Railway but as we have already read, the estates company, the pier and just about everything else that was in fact Lee-on-the-Solent at about that time.

The obituary in *The Times* of April 11th 1913 described Sir John Charles Robinson as an artist and art connoisseur, who had a natural flair for works of art of every description. "As superintendent of the art collections at the Victoria and Albert Museum he did a really great public service by obtaining the unrivalled collections that could never have been what they are had the museum not been served by a man so energetic, shrewd and clever as he was".

An obituary for Charles Newton-Robinson said "He will be remembered for his exceptionally wide range of knowledge and culture and for the many-sidedness of his activities". Apart from his interest in developing Lee-on-the-Solent, he was also involved in a similar development at Tankerton in Kent where he also set up a Tankerton Estate Company.

In 1918 the Admiralty opened a seaplane/searchlight depot near to the station at Lee-on-the-Solent and with temporary sidings laid down there is no doubt that the Railway Company hoped for much extra revenue which unfortunately never really materialised.

On April 20th 1921 the Lee-on-the-Solent Railway Company applied to bring their line under the provisions of the Light Railway Acts of 1896 and 1912 which would relieve them from the obligations contained in the Railway Construction Facilities Act of 1864. Powers were obtained for the line on November 11th 1921 which meant that level crossing gates and their keepers were abolished on May 8th 1922.

Even coming under the Light Railway Acts of 1896 and 1912 did not really help the finances of the Lee-on-the-Solent Railway and they continued to feel the pinch, still finding it hard to cover operating expenses. With the 1923 Grouping Act fast approaching, the debit balance carried forward was now £13,761, while the accrued liabilities were £14,597. The newly formed Southern Railway who were due to absorb the Lee-on-the-Solent Railway under the terms of the Railway Act of 1921 which laid out the framework for the 1923 Grouping were not happy being forced to take on the £14,597 debt and even took the matter before the Railway Amalgamation Tribunal on January 4th 1923. It was agreed by the Tribunal that the Southern Railway should be responsible for the debt and even an appeal a few months later against the decision was dismissed. The following was soon issued:-

"Under the Southern Railway (Lee-on-the-Solent Railway) Absorption Scheme 1923 dated August 11th 1923, Lee-on-the-Solent Railway Company was transferred to and absorbed by the Southern Railway Company from January 1st 1923 and dissolved from August 11th 1923".

There's no doubt the Southern Railway felt that they had taken on a great burden and although they made some attempt to improve things, it was soon obvious that under the new owners, the Lee-on-the-Solent Railway had no future and it came as no surprise when it was announced on April 28th 1930 that due to collecting fares from the few passengers who wanted to travel between the halts, the passenger service between the three halts would be withdrawn. On October 16th 1930 the Southern Railway Traffic and Continental Committee recommended that the line would close throughout to passengers as and on January 1st 1931.

Although closed to passengers, the line did stay open for goods until September 30th 1935 when it was officially closed completely although the last goods train ran on Wednesday October 2nd 1935. (*see pages 27 to 30 for full details of the closures*).

Description of the Route

The station at Fort Brockhurst was opened in May 1865 as Brockhurst which was some 24 years after the line from Bishopstoke (later to be re-named Eastleigh) to Gosport had originally opened on November 29th 1841 although, due to a collapsed tunnel north of Fareham just four days later, the line was closed and finally re-opened on February 7th 1842. When the Lee-on-the Solent Railway opened in 1894, the station became a junction and at about this time was re-named Fort Brockhurst to save confusion with Brockenhurst Station in the New Forest. Like Fort Gomer, Fort Brockhurst was one of several nearby Victorian forts which were known locally as Palmerston's Folly.

The original main station buildings consisted of offices with a substantial residence for the Station Master on the up side while the down side consisted of just a small shelter.

A new bay platform was added at the back of the main up platform for the new line and was approached through a gate from the up platform. There was no shelter provided although passengers for Lee-on-the-Solent could wait in the main station.

The bay consisted of a run-round loop and a headshunt running parallel with the main line from which a connection ran back to a junction with the main line at the southern end of the station. This meant that a shunt move was necessary to place or remove a train on to the Lee-on-the-Solent line.

An early view of the station at Brockhurst looking towards Gosport before the name was changed to Fort Brockhurst and, before the signal box was added and the Lee-on-the-Solent line built. The Garrison Church is on the extreme right of the photograph. National Railway Museum

FORT BROCKHURST STATION

Former LB&SCR "Terrier" No.E735 and a single 'gate' carriage at the bay platform at Fort Brockhurst on November 5th 1928.   H.C.Casserley

LSWR 2-4-0T No.21 "Scott" also at the bay platform at Fort Brockhurst on September 6th 1899. The Garrison Church is on the right.   Author's Collection

From Fort Brockhurst the single track curved away sharply southwards so that before long it was at right angles to the main line and running parallel with Military Road before reaching what was then known as Pound Lane Crossing which was 28 chains from Fort Brockhurst. Local rumour has it that unofficially, the train would sometimes stop to allow schoolchildren to alight for the nearby Garrison School. It must be pointed out that this was to have been one of the stopping places when the original plans were for low platforms at the intermediate stopping places. This crossing which was later called Cambridge Road Crossing was gated until May 8th 1922 when like the other gated crossings on the line, the gates were removed.

From Pound Lane Crossing the line continued for 1 mile 1 chain and curving to the right arrived at Fort Gomer Halt after passing over an adjoining level crossing with its crossing keepers hut. As mentioned in the history of the line, Fort Gomer Halt was originally opened as Privett but, after the LSWR took over the running of the line, they requested that the Lee-on-the-Solent Railway Company changed the name to save confusion with their Privett Station on their Meon Valley line. Fort Gomer being the name of another one of the Victorian forts in the district. The halt consisted of a single platform on the down side and somewhat surprisingly did not have a shelter until after requests from members of the general public in February 1920 one was added at a cost £245.

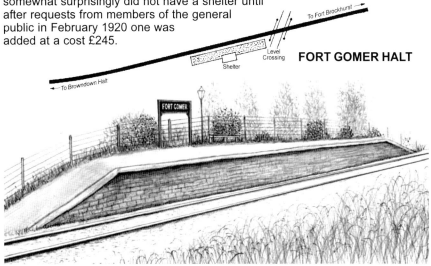

Fort Gomer Halt looking towards Browndown before the shelter was added in February 1920.
From a drawing by the author.

From Fort Gomer Halt the line continued turning towards the west, running over marshy ground on a slight embankment. It was this area which gave the contractors the most trouble while constructing the line. The line then went over the first of two bridges which crossed over two courses of the small River Alver. The first bridge was 1 mile 23 chains from Fort Brockhurst and had an 11 feet 6 inch span with a height of 6 feet 6 inches. The second bridge was 250 yards further on and was identical to the first one. They were constructed of four steel girders on a decking of old rails laid on wooden stringers and supported on piles with concrete abutments.

The line then continued on a right hand curve going through a shallow cutting and passing Browndown Military Camp on the left. It then ran parallel to Military Road which is now known as Privett Road before going over a level crossing and arriving at Browndown Halt which was 1 mile 68 chains from Fort Brockhurst.

The single platform at Browndown was very similar to Fort Gomer and was also on the down side, but unlike Fort Gomer, it never had a shelter even though due to the nearby Browndown Ranges, it probably had more passengers (especially from the armed forces) than any of the other halts between Fort Brockhurst and Lee-on-the-Solent. The nearby ranges included a 2 feet 6 inches gauge tramway system which ran in three sections from a central repairing shop and store to three banks of targets near the shore. A fourth tramway was added by 1931. Not a great deal is known about the working of this tramway although it is thought that the target trucks were hand pushed.

To Fort Gomer Halt ➡

◀ To Elmore Halt

Level Crossing

BROWNDOWN HALT

Browndown Halt, looking towards Fort Gomer.   Lens of Sutton

The line to Lee-on-the-Solent continued from Browndown and ran level with the Portsmouth Road with fine views of the Solent and the Isle of Wight on the left of the line. This continued until the line arrived at Elmore Halt which was 2 miles 45 chains from Fort Brockhurst. The platform at Elmore Halt was on the up side of the line and was opened on April 11th 1910 and had a shelter added in December 1910 at a cost of £32. It seems that Elmore Halt got its name from the nearby Elmore Farm and this was to have been one of the stopping places when the line was first suggested.

Elmore Halt, looking towards Lee-on-the-Solent.   Author's Collection

A closer view of Elmore Halt, looking towards Lee-on-the-Solent.   Author's Collection

From here the line turned in a north west direction and headed towards the terminus at Lee-on-the-Solent. At this point the route followed the Marine Parade and was near to the beach as it ran along the shore and on reaching the terminus at Lee-on-the-Solent the line turned slightly to the left before straightening out again and passed over an ungated level crossing next to a boat house. The station was 3 miles 8 chains from Fort Brockhurst and was situated next to the pier, it comprised of brick built station buildings which were at right angles to the track and buffer stops. The approach for passengers was down a slope from Marine Parade and through a set of large double doors into the building and on to a single platform on the up side without any form of cover. The layout was a single track and run-round loop with a crossover mid-way so that part of the loop could be used as a siding. As there were no signals on the line the points on the running line were unlocked by a key on the train staff. At the other end of the platform from the buildings and adjacent to a small coal stage was a crane and a water tank which was on wooden trestles. Plans for a proposed engine shed and replacement water tank sited on the approach to the station were also drawn up but never built.

In 1918 the Admiralty decided to open a seaplane/searchlight depot near the station and temporary sidings were laid down on the north side to the approach from Elmore. These sidings were later removed in 1922.

Former LB&SCR "Terrier" No.E735 and a single gate carriage at Lee-on-the-Solent Station on November 5th 1928.   H.C.Casserley

21

LEE-ON-THE-SOLENT STATION

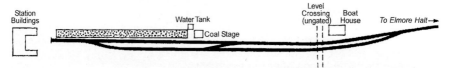

An interesting view of the station buildings at Lee-on-the-Solent.   Author's Collection

Gradient Profile

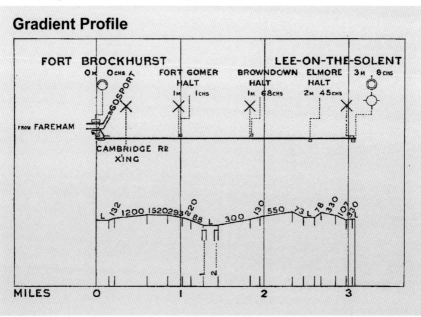

Motive Power and Rolling Stock

As previously mentioned, the locomotive which pulled the first train when the line opened was a Manning Wardle 0-6-0ST locomotive called "Jumbo" which was on loan from the LSWR as the Lee-on-the-Solent Company never in fact owned any locomotives. "Jumbo" had been working on the Bodmin & Wadebridge Railway and it is thought that is where it returned soon after the new railway was opened. Unfortunately, after the condemnation of the firebox, "Jumbo" was broken up in June 1896.

The regular engine in the early days of the line was "Scott" a 2-4-0T built by George England and delivered new to the LSWR in 1861 and was based at Wimbledon permanent way depot as No.15 and received the name "Scott" after the then LSWR's traffic manager Archibald Scott. Transferred to the Locomotive Department in January 1874 and overhauled at Nine Elms in 1875 it later received the number 21.

In 1903, when "Scott" was under repair, the LSWR loaned a locomotive formerly called "Lady Portsmouth" which like "Jumbo" was another Manning Wardle 0-6-0ST. This engine was obtained by the LSWR from the contractor R.T.Relf, who had given it the name "Lady Portsmouth" and number 392. After a visit to the works at Nine Elms in 1885 for a new boiler the name was left off and not replaced.

With the LSWR taking over the running of the line from July 26th 1909, they started using from September 1st 1909 their H13 class Steam Railcars which were designed by Dugald Drummond (the LSWR Locomotive Superintendent from 1895 to 1912). These Railcars had the engine portion encased in the coachwork unlike Drummond's original design which had both the engine and coach mounted on a single underframe. H13 class Steam Railcar No.10 was the first of this type to be used on the line after it had been working on the Bordon Light Railway and the service was then later covered by No.9. The H13 class Steam Railcars only lasted until about 1915 when they were withdrawn and replaced by former London Brighton & South Coast Railway (LB&SCR) "Terrier" class 0-6-0 No.735 originally called "Clapham" and purchased by the LSWR in 1903 and was fitted with auto gear for pull-and-push working.

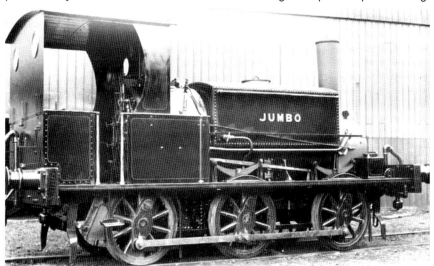

LSWR 0-6-0ST "Jumbo" built by Manning Wardle.   Author's Collection

After the Grouping, there seems to have been a greater choice of locomotives which included the reboilered and rebuilt "Terriers" classified as "A1X". Two of this class No.655 formerly called "Stepney" and No.661 formally called "Sutton" who later gained "B" prefixes to their numbers were fitted with LSWR pattern motor gear and they shared duties on the line with No.735. A Adams O2 class 0-4-4T was also used at one time. The locomotives to work the last few years on the line were former LB&SCR D1 class 0-4-2T's.

As we have previously read, before the line opened, the Company obtained two rather ornate tramway style bogie carriages with longitudinal seats and end platforms. These carriages were built by Brown Marshalls of Birmingham and seated 34 passengers, 10 of which were first class. A 4-wheeled passenger van was also noted as working on the line and this was thought to be No.46, a LSWR brake van built in 1895. After the Steam Railcars had departed, passengers were carried in LSWR 'gate' stock, followed by pull-and-push carriage sets or a single carriage.

LSWR 2-4-0T No.21 "Scott" at Fort Brockhurst on December 26th 1900.   Pamlin Print

LSWR 0-6-0ST No.392 formally called "Lady Portsmouth".   Col Stephens Railway Museum, Tenterden

Former LB&SCR "Terrier" A1X No.B661 at Lee-on-the-Solent on February 14th 1928. H.C.Casserley

H13 class Steam Railcar No.10 which worked on the line in 1909. Author's Collection

O2 class 0-4-4T No.232 at the bay platform at Fort Brockhurst. Author's Collection

Former LB&SCR "Terrier" class 0-6-0 No.E735 purchased by the LSWR in 1903. Author's Collection

Timetables & Tickets

Surprisingly, for a line which hoped to attract passengers to a new seaside resort, the Sunday service was reduced from five trains from Fort Brockhurst when the line opened in 1894, to just three trains in 1908. When the H13 class Steam Railcars were in use, the summer Sunday service increased to five again but with no service during June. The Sunday service seems to have been abandoned by the 1914-18 war and was never re-instated.

Lee-on-the-Solent Railway

TRAIN SERVICE BETWEEN
Lee-on-the-Solent & Fort Brockhurst Junction (L. & S.W.R.)

1st JUNE to 30th SEPTEMBER, 1908 (or until further notice).

FROM LEE-ON-THE-SOLENT

STATIONS		WEEK DAYS.								SUNDAYS.				
		a.m.	a.m.	a.m.	p.m.	p.m.	p.m.	p.m.	p.m.	p.m.	p.m	p.m.	p.m.
Lee-on-the-Solent ...	dep.	9.20	10.35	11.50	2.10	2.50	4.10	6.30	7.30	3.0	4.35	...	6.40
Browndown	..	...	Stop	by	signal			...		Stop	by	signal	
Privett	...	..		do.	do.			...		...	do	do.	
Fort Brockhurst Junction	arr.	9.35	10.50	12. 5	2.25	3. 5	4.25	6.45	7.45	3.15	4.50	...	6.55

TO LEE-ON-THE-SOLENT

		a.m.	a.m.	a.m.	a.m.	p.m.	p.m.	p.m.	p.m.	p.m.	p.m.	p.m.	p.m.	p.m.	p m.
Fort Brockhurst Junction	dep.	10.15	...	11.30	12.55	2.30	3 50	4.55	7. 5	8. 5		4. 5	4.55	7. 0
Privett	...			...	Stop		by	signal			Stop	by	signal	
Browndown	...			...	do.		do.	..			...	do.	do.	
Lee-on-the-Solent	arr.	10.30		11.45	1.10	2.45	4. 5	5.10	7.20	8 20		4.20	5.10	7.15

C Southampton West.   A London Passengers by these Trains, travel via. Meon Valley Line.

NOTICE.—The published Time Tables of the Lee-on-the-Solent Railway Company are only intended to fix the time before which the trains will not start, and the Company do not undertake that the trains shall start or arrive at the time specified in the Tables, nor do they guarantee the connection of trains at the various Junctions. The Company give notice that they will not be responsible for any loss, inconvenience, or expense which may arise from delay or detention, or from non-correspondence of trains at the Junctions. The times of arrival and departure of the L. & S.W. Trains at Fort Brockhurst & other Stations are given for information only & the Lee-on-the-Solent Company do not hold themselves responsible for the accuracy of same.

FARES:—

From Fort Brockhurst to Lee-on-the-Solent & vice versa—1st Class 9d., 2nd Class 6d., 3rd Class 3d.

Through Day Return Tickets are issued from **Lee-on-the-Solent** to **Portsmouth** and vice versa, (via Floating Bridge Co. and Tramway to Station Road, Brockhurst; Passengers should allow 20 minutes from Gosport Hard)—Fares 1st Class 1/11; 2nd Class 1/5; Third Class 10d.

Passengers can also book through to and from Principal L. & S. W. Stations.

E. A. ROBINSON, Manager.

H. W. Duffett, Printer, High Street, Fareham.

FORT BROCKHURST and LEE-ON-THE-SOLENT.—Southern.   1924

Miles		Week Days only.								Miles		Week Days only.							
—	Fort Brockhurst dep.	mrn	mrn	aft	aft	aft	aft	aft	aft		Lee-on-the-Solent dep.	mrn	mrn	aft	aft	aft	aft	aft	aft
—	Fort Brockhurst dep.	9 10	1035	1235	2 45	4	5 4	48 6	15 7 15		Lee-on-the-Solent dep.	9 40	1125	1 10	3 40	4 25	5 15	6 55	7 55
—	Fort Gomer Halt	9 13	1038	1238	2 48	4	5 4	51 6	18 7 18		Elmore Halt.........	9 43	1128	1 13	3 43	4 28	5 18	6 58	7 58
—	Browndown Halt.....	9 18	1043	1243	2 53	4 13	5 6	56 6	23 7 23		Browndown Halt	9 47	1132	1 17	3 47	4 32	5 22	7 2	8 2
—	Elmore Halt.........	9 22	1047	1247	2 57	4 17	5 0	6 27	7 27		Fort Gomer Halt [171	9 51	1136	1 21	3 51	4 36	5 26	7 6	8 6
3	Lee-on-the-Solent arr.	9 26	1051	1251	3 1	4 21	5	4 6	31 7 31	3	Fort Brockhurst arr.	9 56	1141	1 26	3 56	4 41	5 31	7 11	8 11

Closure

The Southern Railway had inherited the line between Fort Brockhurst and Lee-on-the-Solent somewhat reluctantly and although they made some effort to make a go of it, the inevitable happened and after announcing on April 28th 1930 that the passenger service between the three halts would be withdrawn, the announcement came on October 16th 1930 that the line would close for passengers on and from January 1st 1931 meaning that the last passenger train would run the day before on New Year's Eve although, the line would remain open for goods. *The Portsmouth Evening News* of Thursday January 1st 1931 reported the events when former LB&SCR D1 class 0-4-2T No.B626 worked the final passenger service on the last day:-

THE LAST TRAIN FROM LEE
Six Men and a Dog
Farewell handshakes with officials

Six Lee-on-the-Solent men and a dog travelled on the light railway from Lee to Fort Brockhurst and back, with first class tickets on Wednesday, to mark the occasion of the last passenger train on regular service running on this branch line.

The passengers waved to all and sundry as they journeyed along, and onlookers probably wondered what all the fuss was about, maybe forgetting that the day was the finishing day for the service. The young men also sang old-time songs. When nearly home the party were surprised to hear three loud reports as the train passed along the metals. Fog signals had been placed on the line by way of a farewell salute.

Handshaking all round took place when the train came to a standstill. Stationmaster, guard, engine-driver and fireman joined in and the best of good wishes were expressed, including that of "A happy and prosperous New Year".

It is pleasing to note that the officials displaced at Lee are already allotted positions elsewhere with the Railway Company.

In their book *'Steaming to Rainbows End'* authors Mervyn Turvey & David Andrews mention that a Mr.Brewis of Stubbington remembers that he was one of the last passengers on that final run and he was accompanied by three brothers, Russell, Geoffrey and Robert Browning and "Bruno" their silver spaniel. He did not realise that there were any other passengers on that memorable day. When the last train arrived at Fort Brockhurst, he and the three Browning brothers and the dog detrained and walked all the way home.

It's interesting to note that although the *Portsmouth Evening News* mentions six men and a dog, the Friday January 2nd 1931 edition of the *Hampshire Telegraph & Post*, says that there were only four passengers carried on the final run which confirms what Mr.Brewis mentioned. The same paper also mentioned that the advent of the motor omnibus caused a rapid decline in the popularity of the railway and that it became a lonely existence for the driver and fireman with their passengerless trains. The paper then went on to say the following:-

A sad business, but there was one gleam of gladness. Should the time ever come that a writer feels inspired to pen an epic to this gallant little train, he must record that on its final day, it had one glorious hour.

Driver C.Stubbington and Fireman Hoylake were impressed with the weight of responsibility suddenly thrust upon them.

They negotiated the crossings with more care than usual. They whistled their way with caution through the fastnesses of Browndown and they delivered their human cargo safe and sound at the destination.

More than that cannot be demanded of any driver or fireman. The last journey was again without incident. If only a cow had strayed on the line or the engine had kicked up his hind wheels! but nothing happened and the Gosport - Lee express passed out, "Unwept, unhonoured, unsung".

The final day of passenger service at Lee-on-the-Solent. D1 class 0-4-2T No.B626 and LSWR 'gate' set No.374 wait at the platform on December 31st 1930. Left to right:- E.Perkins (carriers), W.Foster (guard), M.Serle (Gosport stationmaster), F.J.Marlow (Lee-on-the-Solent staff), Fireman (unknown), V.H.Bricknell (driver). *Portsmouth Evening News*

(*Left*) F.J.Marlow shakes the hand of driver V.H.Bricknell while the fireman and W.Foster the guard look on. (*Right*) The train waits at the Lee-on-the-Solent platform on the last day. Portsmouth Evening News

Although now closed for passengers, the line continued working for goods from and to Fort Brockhurst and its interesting to note that during 1933 a daily goods train still served the line. The main requirements being coal, building materials and supplies for the nearby naval air station, the staff required for loading and unloading travelling in the brake van. From about this time it seems that it became an 'as required service' and maybe not such a great surprise when the official announcement was made by the Southern Railway that the goods line between Fort Brockhurst and Lee-on-the-Solent would close on and after Monday September 30th 1935 and that the station at Lee-on-the-Solent would also close.

Although the official date of closure was given as September 30th 1935, the actual last goods train ran on Wednesday October 2nd 1935 and the Friday October 4th 1935 edition of the *Hampshire Telegraph & Post* described proceedings when former LB&SCR D1 class 0-4-2T No.2239 pulled the final goods train, as follows:-

THE LEE-BROCKHURST GOODS TRAIN'S FINAL RUN

So far as the railway is concerned, Lee-on-the-Solent is now "off the map". No more will the echoes resound with the shriek of the whistle and the popping of the fussy little engine which has daily dragged a goods train from Brockhurst to Lee and back again, for that goods train has left the quaint collection of buildings bearing the dignified title Lee Railway Station for the last time, carrying with it the safe, clock and other office furniture, as well as the station lamp and barrow.

For the last time, Mr.F.J.Marlow who for 13 years has been stationmaster, booking clerk, ticket collector, porter and lamp boy all rolled into one, locked the station doors, and joined Mr.M.Searle, Stationmaster at Gosport (whose administrative area includes Lee), and Mr.W.Foster, the guard, and made the journey to Brockhurst, at the end of a 16-truck train, in a brake van on Wednesday.

Mr.V.H.Bricknell, the engine driver, had been making the journey daily for 23 years. It fell to his lot to drive the last passenger train in 1930.

"Things Have Changed"

"We had a good service in the early days", he said, whilst "grooming" the engine, in preparation for his last journey. "I have known as many as 30 trains on a Bank Holiday. Things have changed". With a sad gesture he pulled out a piece of cotton waste, and wiped moisture from his hand.

But if he felt sad at this last phase of the change, he hid his feelings, for he tore the peace and quietude of Lee with a special fanfare on the engine whistle, and shattered it with a series of ear-splitting explosions from foghorn signals.

Thus closed a railway which has been in existence for nearly 45 years.

It's interesting to note that this report mentions that it fell to Mr.V.H.Bricknell's lot to drive the last passenger train on December 31st 1930 as the Friday January 2nd 1931 edition of the *Hampshire Telegraph & Post* says that Driver C.Stubbington and Fireman Hoylake had the responsibility of handling the last passenger train. Certainly Mr. Bricknell did drive at sometime on the last day and appears in the photographs on the opposite page.

D1 class 0-4-2T No.2239 with the final goods train at Lee-on-the-Solent on Wednesday October 2nd 1935 with driver V.H.Bricknell on the footplate.   Lens of Sutton

(*Left*) A closer view of Driver V.H.Bricknell on the footplate. (*Right*) The last goods train waits at the platform at Lee-on-the-Solent before leaving for the last time. Portsmouth Evening News

Once the line had officially closed, for some years the track surprisingly remained in position as far as the approach to Elmore Halt and when the late railway photographer R.F.Roberts visited the line in August 1938 they were still there (see photos below). Even when most of the track was finally removed, it is known that until the early 1950's, about ½ mile of the line from Fort Brockhurst remained in use for coal traffic for C.H.House & Sons Limited at Privett Farm.

A derelict Browndown Halt looking towards Fort Gomer in August 1938.

Stephenson Locomotive Society./R.F.Roberts

The end of the line on the approach to Elmore Halt looking back to Browndown in August 1938.

Stephenson Locomotive Society./R.F.Roberts

The Present Scene

Very little evidence remains of the line apart from the original station building at Lee-on-the-Solent which is now Olympia Amusements and although odd bits and pieces of the route can just about be made out, most of it has vanished without trace.

In many ways like the railway, the pier also struggled and although a regular eight trips ran daily between Lee-on-the-Solent and Clarence Pier, Southsea, the main steamer companies in the area did not call. In 1932 a fire destroyed the pavilion at the far end of the pier which was never rebuilt. In 1939 the pier was breached by the military as part of the coastal defence and was never repaired and the remaining structure was demolished in 1958.

In 1935 the Lee Tower complex was constructed on the seafront near to the pier and old station, and the Art Deco building became quite a landmark comprising of a white tower and clock with a 120ft high observation deck, a cinema, ballroom, restaurant, lounge and a saloon bar. Like the pier in 1939 it was also commandeered by the military. The Lee Tower complex did reopen after the war but was never a great success, the cinema closing in 1958 and the whole development being demolished in 1971.

The original seaplane/searchlight depot which was opened in 1918 was later greatly expanded in 1938 to become HMS Daedalus. From 1959 it became HMS Ariel and then in 1965 it again became HMS Daedalus. It has now closed and at the time of writing the site is due for development which hopefully will create much employment for the area.

The former bay platform at Fort Brockhurst Station in March 2006. Nick Catford

The remains of Fort Gomer Halt in 1961 during demolition for road development. Author's Collection

The former station building at Lee-on-the-Solent on April 14th 2011. Author

Conclusion

Although the railway was seen as an important part of the development of Lee-on-the-Solent as a seaside resort, it never really reached the original hopes of the promoters. The fact that it was always just a shuttle service rattling backwards and forwards between Fort Brockhurst and Lee and was very much a light railway with no direct connection with the main line without a shunt move over a siding, it quickly noticed competition from improving road transport. Perhaps if the promoters had pushed more for the direct line from Fareham via Titchfield and Crofton which was the original idea in 1888 it may have stood a better chance.

Like so many similar branch lines and light railways which have now disappeared from our landscape, if it had survived it would no doubt be a great tourist attraction today and even more, just imagine how useful it would have been as a transport link to the HMS Daedalus site.

Looking back, one wonders what the reaction would be if Charles Newton-Robinson and his father Sir John Charles Robinson could see what Lee-on-the-Solent and the area is like today.

Acknowledgements

My sincere thanks to the following people and organisations for their kind help in compiling information and supplying photographs for this publication: R.M.Casserley for the H.C.Casserley photographs, John Alsop for supplying photographs from his interesting collection, the Stephenson Locomotive Society for the R.F.Roberts photographs, the librarians and staff at Portsmouth, Gosport and Lee-on-the-Solent libraries and Gerald Jacobs. Thanks to Douglas Stuckey for suggesting the subject and for all his encouragement and to Norman Branch for reading my text. Finally, thanks to James Christian and Dan Perkins of Binfield Print & Design for their help.

Bibliography

THE RAILWAYS OF GOSPORT by Kevin Robertson (Noddle Books)
BRANCH LINES AROUND GOSPORT by Vic Mitchell & Keith Smith (Middleton Press)
THE HIDDEN RAILWAYS OF PORTSMOUTH & GOSPORT by Dave Marden (Kestrel Books)
RAILWAY ARCHIVE - The Lee-on-the-Solent Railway by John Alsop (Lightmoor Press)
RAILS TO THE TOWER by Peter Keat (Gosport Railway Society)
STEAMING TO RAINBOWS END by Mervyn Turvey & David Andrews (Lee Press)

A post-war view of the railway trackbed at the site of Elmore Halt looking towards Lee-on-the-Solent. The breached pier can be just be seen on the left of the photograph. John Alsop Collection